*Helen
Steiner Rice*

A
COLLECTION OF
COMFORT

BARBOUR
PUBLISHING

A HELEN STEINER RICE ® Product

© 2013 by Barbour Publishing, Inc.

All poems © Helen Steiner Rice Foundation Fund, LLC, a wholly owned subsidiary of Cincinnati Museum Center. All rights reserved.

Published under license from the Helen Steiner Rice Foundation Fund, LLC.

Print ISBN 978-1-62069-159-7

eBook Editions:
Adobe Digital Edition (.epub) 978-1-62029-700-1
Kindle and MobiPocket Edition (.prc) 978-1-62029-699-8

Published by Barbour Publishing, Inc., P.O. Box 719, Uhrichsville, Ohio 44683, www.barbourbooks.com

Our mission is to publish and distribute inspirational products offering exceptional value and biblical encouragement to the masses.

 Member of the
Evangelical Christian
Publishers Association

Printed in the United States of America.

CONTENTS

LINES OF
ENCOURAGEMENT

THE HAND OF
GOD IS EVERYWHERE

It's true we have never looked on His face,
But His likeness shines forth from every place,
For the hand of God is everywhere
Along life's busy thoroughfare,
And His presence can be felt and seen
Right in the midst of our daily routine.
Things we touch and see and feel
Are what make God so very real.

Do Not Be Anxious

Do not be anxious, said our Lord;
Have peace from day to day—
The lilies neither toil nor spin,
Yet none are clothed as they.
The meadowlark with sweetest song
Fears not for bread or nest
Because he trusts our Father's love
And God knows what is best.

GIVE LAVISHLY!
LIVE ABUNDANTLY!

The more you give, the more you get.
The more you laugh, the less you fret.
The more you do unselfishly,
The more you live abundantly.
The more of everything you share,
The more you'll always have to spare.
The more you love, the more you'll find
That life is good and friends are kind,
For only what we give away
Enriches us from day to day.

NEVER BE DISCOURAGED

There is really nothing we need know
or even try to understand
If we refuse to be discouraged
and trust God's guiding hand.
So take heart and meet each minute
with faith in God's great love,
Aware that every day of life
is controlled by God above.
And never dread tomorrow
or what the future brings,
Just pray for strength and courage
and trust God in all things.
And never grow discouraged—
be patient and just wait,
For God never comes too early,
and He never comes too late.

In Hours of Discouragement, God Is Our Encouragement

Sometimes we feel uncertain
and unsure of everything,
Afraid to make decisions,
dreading what the day will bring.
We keep wishing it were possible
to dispel all fear and doubt
And to understand more readily
just what life is all about.
God has given us the answers,
which too often go unheeded,
But if we search His promises
we'll find everything that's needed. . .
For in God is our encouragement
in trouble and in trials,
And in suffering and in sorrow
He will turn our tears to smiles.

SEEK FIRST THE KINGDOM OF GOD

Life is a mixture of sunshine and rain,
Good things and bad things, pleasure and pain.
We can't have all sunshine, but it's certainly true
That there's never a cloud
the sun doesn't shine through. . .
Take heart and stand tall and think who you are,
For God is your Father and no one can bar
Or keep you from reaching your desired success
Or withhold the joy that is yours to possess. . .
For you need nothing more
than God's guidance and love
To ensure you the things
that you're most worthy of. . .
So trust in His wisdom and follow His ways
And be not concerned with the world's empty praise,
But first seek His kingdom and you will possess
The world's greatest of riches,
which is true happiness.

IF YOU MEET GOD IN THE MORNING. . .

Each day at dawning I lift my heart high
And raise up my eyes to the infinite sky.
I watch the night vanish as a new day is born,
And I hear the birds sing on the wings of the morn.
I see the dew glisten in crystal-like splendor,
While God, with a touch that is gentle and tender,
Wraps up the night and softly tucks it away
And hangs out the sun to herald a new day. . .
And so I give thanks and my heart kneels to pray,
"God, keep me and guide me
and go with me today."

YOUR LIFE WILL BE BLESSED
IF YOU LOOK FOR THE BEST

It's easy to grow downhearted
when nothing goes your way.
It's easy to be discouraged
when you have a troublesome day.
But trouble is only a challenge
to spur you on to achieve
The best that God has to offer,
if you have the faith to believe!

TODAY, TOMORROW, AND ALWAYS, HE IS THERE

In sickness or health,
In suffering and pain,
In storm-laden skies,
In sunshine and rain,
God always is there
To lighten your way
And lead you through darkness
To a much brighter day.

A Sure Way
to a Happy Day

Happiness is something we create in our minds;
It's not something you search for
and so seldom find.
It's just waking up and beginning the day
By counting our blessings and kneeling to pray.
It's giving up thoughts that breed discontent
And accepting what comes as a gift heaven sent.
It's giving up wishing for things we have not
And making the best of whatever we've got.
It's knowing that life is determined for us
And pursuing our tasks
without fret, fume, or fuss. . .
For it's by completing what God gives us to do
That we find real contentment and happiness, too.

SPIRITUAL STRENGTH

Life can't always be a song;
You have to have trouble to make you strong.
So whenever you are troubled
and everything goes wrong,
It is just God working in you
to make your spirit strong.

GOD'S STAIRWAY

Step by step we climb day by day
Closer to God with each prayer we pray,
For the cry of the heart offered in prayer
Becomes just another spiritual stair
In the heavenly place where we live anew. . .
So never give up, for it's worth the climb
To live forever in endless time,
Where the soul of man is safe and free
To live and love through eternity.

INSPIRATION! MEDITATION! DEDICATION!

*B*righten your day
And lighten your way
And lessen your cares
With daily prayers.
Quiet your mind
And leave tension behind
And find inspiration
In hushed meditation.

TROUBLE IS A STEPPING STONE TO GROWTH

*T*rouble is something no one can escape—
Everyone has it in some form or shape.
Some people hide it way down deep inside;
Some people bear it with gallant-like pride.
Some people worry and complain of their lot;
Some people covet what they haven't got.
But the wise man accepts whatever God sends,
Willing to yield like a storm-tossed tree bends,
Knowing that God never made a mistake,
So whatever He sends they are willing to take. . .
For trouble is part and parcel of life,
And no man can grow without struggle or strife.
So blessed are the people who learn to accept
The trouble men try to escape and reject,
For in accordance we're given great grace
And courage and faith and strength to face
The daily troubles that come to us all,
So we may learn to stand straight and tall. . .
For the grandeur of life is born of defeat,
For in overcoming we make like complete.

Be Glad

Be glad that your life has been full and complete;
Be glad that you've tasted the bitter and sweet.
Be glad that you've walked in sunshine and rain;
Be glad that you've felt both pleasure and pain.
Be glad that you've had such a full, happy life;
Be glad for your joy as well as your strife.
Be glad that you've walked with courage each day;
Be glad you've had strength for each step of the way.
Be glad for the comfort that you've found in prayer.
Be glad for God's blessings, His love, and His care.

Assurance of God's Love

God's Keeping

To be in God's keeping is surely a blessing,
For though life is often dark and distressing,
No day is too dark and no burden too great
That God in His love cannot penetrate.

In God Is Our Strength

*I*t's a troubled world we live in,
and we wish that we might find
Not only happiness of heart
but longed-for peace of mind. . .
But where can we begin our search
in the age of automation,
With neighbor against neighbor
and nation against nation,
Where values have no permanence
and change is all around,
And everything is sinking sand
and nothing solid ground?
But we've God's Easter promise,
so let us seek a goal
That opens up new vistas
for man's eternal soul. . .
For our strength and our security
lie not in earthly things
But in Christ the Lord, who died for us
and rose as King of kings.

WITH HIS LOVE

If you found any beauty in the poems in this book
or some peace and comfort in a word or a line,
Don't give me the praise or the worldly acclaim,
for the words that you read are not mine.
I borrowed them all to share with you
from our heavenly Father above,
And the joy that you felt was God speaking to you
as He flooded your heart with His love.

No Favor Do
I Seek Today

I come not to ask,
to plead or implore You—
I just come to tell You
how much I adore You.
For to kneel in Your presence
makes me feel blessed,
For I know that You
know all my needs best,
And it fills me with joy
just to linger with You
As my soul You replenish
and my heart You renew.
For prayer is much more
than just asking for things—
It's the peace and contentment
that quietness brings.
So thank You again
for Your mercy and love
And for making me heir
to Your kingdom above.

God's Assurance
Gives Us Endurance

My blessings are so many,
my troubles are so few,
How can I be discouraged
when I know that I have You?
And I have the sweet assurance
that there's nothing I need fear
If I but keep remembering
I am Yours and You are near.
Help me to endure the storms
that keep raging deep inside me,
And make me more aware each day
that no evil can betide me.
If I remain undaunted
though the billows sweep and roll,
Knowing I have Your assurance,
there's a haven for my soul,
For anything and everything
can somehow be endured
If Your presence is beside me
and lovingly assured.

What Is Love?

*W*hat is love? No words can define it—
It's something so great only God could design it.
Wonder of wonders, beyond man's conception—
And only in God can love find true perfection. . .
For love means much more
than small words can express,
For what man calls love is so very much less
Than the beauty and depth and the true richness of
God's gift to mankind of compassion from above
For love has become a word that's misused,
Perverted, distorted, and often abused
But love is enduring and patient and kind—
It judges all with the heart, not with the mind. . .
It's faithful and trusting and always believing,
Guileless and honest and never deceiving.
Yes, love is beyond what man can define,
For love is immortal and God's gift is divine!

Not What You Want, but What God Wills

Do you want what you want when you want it,
do you pray and expect a reply?
And when it's not instantly answered,
do you feel that God passed you by?
Well, prayers that are prayed in this manner
are really not prayers at all,
For you can't go to God in a hurry
and expect Him to answer your call.
For prayers are not meant for obtaining
what we selfishly wish to acquire,
For God in His wisdom refuses
the things that we wrongly desire. . .
And don't pray for freedom from trouble
or pray that life's trials pass you by.
Instead pray for strength and for courage
to meet life's dark hours and not cry
That God was not there when you called Him
and He turned a deaf ear to your prayer
And just when you need Him most of all
He left you alone in despair.

GOD'S HAND
IS ALWAYS THERE

I am perplexed and often vexed,
And sometimes I cry and sadly sigh,
But do not think, dear Father above,
That I question You or Your unfailing love.
It's just that sometimes when I reach out,
You seem to be nowhere about,
And while I'm sure You love me still,
I know in my heart that You always will,
Somehow I feel I cannot reach You,
And though I get on my knees and beseech You,
I cannot bring You close to me,
And I feel adrift on life's raging sea. . .
But though I cannot find Your hand
To lead me on to the promised land,
I still believe with all my being
Your hand is still there beyond my seeing.

WARM OUR HEARTS WITH THY LOVE

Oh, God, who made the summer
and warmed the earth with beauty,
Warm our hearts with gratitude
and devotion to our duty. . .
For in this age of violence,
rebellion, and defiance,
We've forgotten the true meaning
of dependable reliance. . .
Our standards have been lowered,
and we resist all discipline,
And our vision has been narrowed
and blinded to all sin.
Oh, put the summer brightness
in our closed, unseeing eyes,
So in the careworn faces
that we pass we'll recognize
The heartbreak and the loneliness,
the trouble and despair
That a word of understanding
would make easier to bear.
Oh God, look down on our cold hearts
and warm them with Your love,
And grant us Your forgiveness
which we're so unworthy of.

GOD'S LOVE IS A HAVEN IN THE STORMS OF LIFE

God's love is like an island
in life's ocean vast and wide,
A peaceful, quiet shelter
from the restless, rising tide.
God's love is like a fortress,
and we seek protection there
When the waves of tribulation
seem to drown us in despair.
God's love is a sanctuary
where our souls can find sweet rest
From the struggle and the tension
of life's fast and futile quest.
God's love is like a tower rising far above the crowd,
And God's smile is like the sunshine
breaking through the threatening cloud.
God's love is like a beacon
burning bright with faith and prayer,
And through all the changing scenes of life
we can find a haven there.

GOD BLESS YOU AND KEEP YOU IN HIS CARE

*T*here are many things in life
we cannot understand,
But we must trust God's judgment
and be guided by His hand. . .
And all who have God's blessing
can rest safely in His care,
For He promises safe passage
on the wings of faith and prayer.

HE LOVES YOU

It's amazing and incredible,
but it's as true as it can be—
God loves and understands us all,
and that means you and me.
His grace is all-sufficient
for both the young and old,
For the lonely and the timid,
for the brash and for the bold.
His love knows no exceptions,
so never feel excluded,
No matter who or what you are,
your name has been included. . .
And no matter what your past has been,
trust God to understand,
And no matter what your problem is,
just place it in His hand. . .
For in all our unloveliness
this great God loves us still—
He loved us since the world began,
and what's more, He always will!

ENFOLDED IN HIS LOVE

The love of God surrounds us
Like the air we breathe around us,
As near as a heartbeat,
as close as a prayer,
And whenever we need Him,
He'll always be there!

You Are
Never Alone

⧜

I Do Not Go Alone

If Death should beckon me
with outstretched hand
And whisper softly
of an unknown land,
I shall not be afraid to go,
For though the path I do not know,
I take Death's hand without fear,
For He who safely brought me here
Will also take me safely back.
And though in many things I lack,
He will not let me go alone
Into the valley that's unknown. . .
So I reach out and take Death's hand
And journey to the Promised Land.

The Heavenly
Staircase

*P*rayers are the stairs that lead to God,
and there's joy every step of the way
When we make our pilgrimage to Him
with love in our hearts each day.

POWER OF PRAYER

I am only a worker employed by the Lord,
And great is my gladness and rich my reward
If I can just spread the wonderful story
That God is the answer to eternal glory. . .
Bringing new hope and comfort and cheer,
Telling sad hearts there is nothing to fear,
And what greater joy could there be than to share
The love of God and the power of prayer.

GOD IS NEVER
BEYOND OUR REACH

No one ever sought the Father
and found He was not there,
And no burden is too heavy
to be lightened by a prayer.
No trials and tribulations
are beyond what we can bear
If we share them with our Father
as we talk to Him in prayer. . .
God asks for no credentials—
He accepts us with our flaws.
He is kind and understanding
and He welcomes us because
We are His erring children
and He loves us, every one,
And He freely and completely
forgives all that we have done,
Asking only if we're ready
to follow where He leads,
Content that in His wisdom
He will answer all our needs.

YOU ARE NEVER ALONE

There's truly nothing we need know
If we have faith wherever we go,
God will be there to help us bear
Our disappointments, pain, and care,
For He is our shepherd, our Father, our guide,
You're never alone with the Lord at your side.

EVERYWHERE ACROSS THE LAND YOU SEE GOD'S FACE AND TOUCH HIS HAND

Each time you look up in the sky,
Or watch the fluffy clouds drift by,
Or feel the sunshine, warm and bright,
Or watch the dark night turn to light,
Or hear a bluebird brightly sing,
Or see the winter turn to spring,
Or stop to pick a daffodil,
Or gather violets on some hill,
Or touch a leave or see a tree,
It's all God whispering, "This is Me. . .
And I am faith and I am light
And in Me there shall be no night."

GOD IS ALWAYS THERE TO HEAR OUR SMALLEST PRAYER

Let us find joy
in the news of His birth,
And let us find comfort
and strength for each day
In knowing that Christ
walked this same earthly way,
So He knows all our needs,
and He hears every prayer,
And He keeps all His children
always safe in His care. . .
And whenever we're troubled
and lost in despair,
We have but to seek Him
and ask Him in prayer
To guide and direct us
and help us to bear
Our sickness and sorrow,
our worry and care. . .
So once more at Christmas
let the whole world rejoice
In the knowledge He answers
every prayer that we voice.

A Part of Me

Dear God, You are a part of me—
You're all I do and all I see;
You're what I say and what I do,
For all my life belongs to You.
You walk with me and talk with me,
For I am Yours eternally,
And when I stumble, slip, and fall
Because I'm weak and lost and small,
You help me up and take my hand
And lead me toward the Promised Land.
I cannot dwell apart from You—
You would not ask or want me to,
For You have room within Your heart
To make each child of Yours a part
Of You and all Your love and care
If we but come to You in prayer.

Worry No More— God Knows the Score

Have you ever been caught
in a web you didn't weave,
Involved in conditions
that are hard to believe?
Have you ever felt you must speak
and explain and deny
A story that's groundless
or a small, whispered lie?
Well, don't be upset,
for God knows the score,
And with God as your judge
you need worry no more...
And secure in this knowledge,
let your thoughts rise above
Man's small, shallow judgments
that are so empty of
God's goodness and greatness
in judging men,
And forget ugly rumors
and be happy again.

MY GOD IS NO STRANGER

God is no stranger in a faraway place;
He's as close as the wind that blows 'cross my face.
It's true I can't see the wind as it blows,
But I feel it around me, and my heart surely knows
That God's mighty hand can be felt everywhere,
For there's nothing on earth that is not in God's care.
The sky and the stars, the waves and the sea,
The dew on the grass, the leaves on a tree
Are constant reminders of God and His nearness,
Proclaiming His presence with crystal-like clearness.
So how could I think God was far, far away
When I feel Him beside me every hour of the day?
And I've plenty of reasons to know God's my friend,
And this is one friendship that time cannot end.

In Him We Live and Move and Have Our Being

We walk in a world that is strange and unknown,
And in the midst of the crowd we still feel alone.
We question our purpose, our part, and our place
In this vast land of mystery suspended in space.
We probe and explore and try hard to explain
The tumult of thoughts that our minds entertain,
But all of our problems and complex explanations
Of man's inner feelings and fears and frustrations
Still leave us engulfed in the mystery of life
With all of its struggles and suffering and strife,
Unable to fathom what tomorrow will bring,
But there is one truth to which we can cling. . .
For while life's a mystery man can't understand,
The great Giver of life is holding our hands,
And safe in His care there is no need for seeing,
"For in Him we live and move and have our being."

CASTING CARES

THE HOUSE OF PRAYER

Just close your eyes and open your heart
And feel your cares and worries depart.
Just yield yourself to the Father above
And let Him hold you secure in His love...
So when you are tired, discouraged, and blue,
There's always one door that is opened to you,
And that is the door to the house of prayer,
And you'll find God waiting to meet you there...
And the house of prayer is no farther away
Than the quiet spot where you kneel and pray.
For the heart is a temple when God is there
As we place ourselves in His loving care...
And He hears every prayer and answers each one
When we pray in His name, "Thy will be done."
And the burdens that seemed too heavy to bear
Are lifted away on the wings of prayer.

Put Your Problems in God's Hands for He Completely Understands

Although it sometimes seems to us
our prayers have not been heard,
God always knows our every need
without a single word,
And He will not forsake us
even though the way is steep,
For always He is near to us,
a tender watch to keep. . .
And in good time He will answer us,
and in His love He'll send
Greater things than we have asked
and blessings without end. . .
So though we do not understand
why trouble comes to man,
Can we not be contented
just to know it is God's plan?

Talk It Over with God

You're worried and troubled about everything,
Wondering and fearing what tomorrow will bring.
You long to tell someone, for you feel so alone,
But your friends are all burdened
with cares of their own.
There is only one place and only one Friend
Who is never too busy, and you can always depend
On Him to be waiting, with arms open wide
To hear all the troubles you came to confide. . .
For the heavenly Father will always be there
When you seek Him and find Him
at the altar of prayer.

WHY AM I COMPLAINING?

My cross is not too heavy,
my road is not too rough
Because God walks beside me,
and to know this is enough. . .
And though I get so lonely,
I know I'm not alone,
For the Lord God is my Father,
and He loves me as His own. . .
So though I'm tired and weary,
and I wish my race were run,
God will only terminate it
when my work on earth is done. . .
So let me stop complaining
about my load of care,
For God will always lighten it
when it gets too much to bear. . .
And if He does not ease my load,
He'll give me strength to bear it,
For God, in love and mercy,
is always near to share it.

ON THE WINGS
OF PRAYER

On the wings of prayer our burdens take flight,
And our load of care becomes bearably light,
And our heavy hearts are lifted above
To be healed by the balm of God's wonderful love. . .
And the tears in our eyes are dried by the hands
Of a loving Father who understands
All of our problems, our fears and despair,
When we take them to Him on the wings of prayer.

GOD WILL NOT FAIL YOU

When life seems empty
and there's no place to go,
When your heart is troubled
and your spirits are low,
When friends seem few
and nobody cares,
There is always God
to hear your prayers. . .
And whatever you're facing
will seem much less
When you go to God
and confide and confess,
For the burden that seems
too heavy to bear
God lifts away
on the wings of prayer. . .
So go to our Father
when troubles assail you,
For His grace is sufficient
and He'll never fail you.

Renewal

When life has lost its luster
and it's filled with dull routine,
When you long to run away from it,
seeking pastures new and green,
Remember, no one runs away from life
without finding when they do
That you can't escape the thoughts you think
that are pressing down on you—
So when your heart is heavy
and your day is dull with care,
Instead of trying to escape,
why not withdraw in prayer?
For in prayer there is renewal
of the spirit, mind, and heart,
For everything is lifted up
in which God has a part—
For when we go to God in prayer,
our thoughts are rearranged,
So even though our problems
have not been solved or changed,
Somehow the good Lord gives us
the power to understand
That He who holds tomorrow
is the One who holds our hands.

LET NOT YOUR
HEART BE TROUBLED

Whenever I am troubled
and lost in deep despair,
I bundle all my troubles up
and go to God in prayer. . .
I tell Him I am heartsick
and lost and lonely, too,
That my mind is deeply burdened,
and I don't know what to do. . .
But I know He stilled the tempest
and calmed the angry sea,
And I humbly ask if, in His love,
He'll do the same for me. . .
And then I just keep quiet
and think only thoughts of peace,
And if I abide in stillness,
my restless murmurings cease.

THE MYSTERY OF PRAYER

*B*eyond that which words can interpret
or theology explain,
The soul feels a shower of refreshment
that falls like the gentle rain
On hearts that are parched with problems
and are searching to find the way
To somehow attract God's attention
through well-chosen words as they pray,
Not knowing that God in His wisdom
can sense all man's worry and woe,
For there is nothing man can conceal
that God does not already know. . .
So kneel in prayer in His presence
and you'll find no need to speak,
For softly in quiet communion,
God grants you the peace that you seek.

ANYWHERE IS A PLACE OF PRAYER IF GOD IS THERE

I have prayed in a velvet, hushed forest,
where the quietness calmed my fears;
I have prayed through suffering and heartache,
when my eyes were blinded with tears.
I have prayed in churches and chapels,
cathedrals and synagogues, too,
But often I had the feeling
that my prayers were not getting through. . .
And I realized then that our Father
is not really concerned when we pray
Or impressed by our manner of worship
or the eloquent words that we say.
He is only concerned with our feelings,
and He looks deep into our hearts
And hears the cry of our souls' deep need
that no words could ever impart. . .
So it isn't the prayer that's expressive
or offered in some special spot
That's the sincere plea of a sinner,
and God can tell whether or not
We honestly seek His forgiveness
and earnestly mean what we say,
And then and then only God answers
the prayers that we fervently pray.

LET DAILY PRAYERS
DISSOLVE YOUR CARES

We all have cares and problems
we cannot solve alone,
But if we go to God in prayer,
we are never on our own.
And no day is unmeetable if,
on rising, our first thought
Is to thank God for the blessings
that His loving care has brought,
For there can be no failures
or hopeless, unsaved sinners
If we enlist the help of God,
who makes all losers winners. . .
And if you follow faithfully
this daily way to pray,
You will never in your lifetime
face another hopeless day. . .
For like a soaring eagle,
you too can rise above
The storms of life around you
on the wings of prayer and love.

ANXIOUS PRAYERS

When we are deeply disturbed by a problem
and our minds are filled with doubt,
And we struggle to find a solution
but there seems to be no way out,
We futilely keep on trying
to untangle our web of distress,
But our own little, puny efforts
meet with very little success.
We kneel down in sheer desperation
and slowly and stumblingly pray,
Then impatiently wait for an answer
in one sudden instant, we say,
"God does not seem to be listening,
so why should we bother to pray?"
But God can't get through to the anxious,
who are much too impatient to wait,
You have to believe in God's promise
that He comes not too soon or too late,
For whether God answers promptly
or delays in answering your prayer,
You must have faith to believe Him
and to know in your heart He'll be there.
So be not impatient or hasty,
just trust in the Lord and believe,
For whatever you ask in faith and love,
in abundance you are sure to receive.

It's Me Again, God

Remember me, God?
I come every day
Just to talk with You, Lord,
and to learn how to pray.
You make me feel welcome;
You reach out Your hand.
I need never explain,
for You understand.
I come to You frightened
and burdened with care,
So lonely and lost
and so filled with despair,
And suddenly, Lord,
I'm no longer afraid—
My burden is lighter
and the dark shadows fade.
Oh, God, what a comfort
to know that You care
And to know when I seek You,
You will always be there.

GIVING COMFORT
TO OTHERS

On Life's Busy Thoroughfares We Meet with Angels Unawares

*T*he unexpected kindness
from an unexpected place,
A hand outstretched in friendship,
a smile on someone's face,
A word of understanding
spoken in a time of trial
Are unexpected miracles
that make life more worthwhile.
For God has many messengers
we fail to recognize,
But He sends them when we need them,
and His ways are wondrous and wise. . .
So keep looking for an angel
and keep listening to hear,
For on life's busy, crowded streets,
you will find God's presence near.

THE GIFT OF FRIENDSHIP

Friendship is a priceless gift
that cannot be bought or sold,
But its value is far greater
than a mountain made of gold—
For gold is cold and lifeless,
it can neither see nor hear,
And in the time of trouble
it is powerless to cheer.
It has no ears to listen,
no heart to understand;
It cannot bring you comfort
or reach out a helping hand—
So when you ask God for a gift,
be thankful if He sends
Not diamonds, pearls, or riches,
but the love of real, true friends.

BRIGHTEN THE CORNER
WHERE YOU ARE

We cannot all be famous
or listed in *Who's Who*,
But every person, great or small,
has important work to do. . .
For seldom do we realize
the importance of small deeds
Or to what degree of greatness
unnoticed kindness leads. . .
So do not sit and idly wish
for wider, new dimensions
Where you can put in practice
your many good intentions,
But at the spot God placed you,
begin at once to do
Little things to brighten up
the lives surrounding you. . .
For if everybody brightened up
the spot on which they're standing
By being more considerate
and a little less demanding,
This dark, old world would
very soon eclipse the evening star
If everybody brightened up
the corner where they are.

WINGS OF LOVE

The priceless gift of life is love,
For with the help of God above
Love can change the human race
And make this world a better place. . .
For love dissolves all hate and fear
And makes our vision bright and clear
So we can see and rise above
Our pettiness on wings of love.

HEART GIFTS

It's not the things that can be bought
That are life's richest treasures;
It's just the little "heart gifts"
That money cannot measure.
A cheerful smile, a friendly word,
A sympathetic nod,
All priceless little treasures
From the storehouse of our God.
They are the things that can't be bought
With silver or with gold,
For thoughtfulness and kindness
And love are never sold.
They are the priceless things in life
For which no one can pay,
And the giver finds rich recompense
In giving them away.

DISCOURAGMENT AND DREAMS

So many things in the line of duty
Drain us of effort and leave us no beauty,
And the dust of the soul grows thick and unswept;
The spirit is drenched in tears unwept.
But just as we fall beside the road,
Discouraged with life
and bowed down with our load,
We lift our eyes, and what seemed a dead end
Is the street of dreams where we meet a friend.

TAKE TIME TO BE KIND

*K*indness is a virtue given by the Lord—
It pays dividends in happiness
and joy is its reward.
For if you practice kindness
in all you say and do,
The Lord will wrap His kindness
around your heart and you.

FRIENDS ARE LIFE'S
GIFT OF LOVE

If people like me didn't know people like you,
Life would lose its meaning and its richness, too. . .
For the friends that we make are life's gift of love,
And I think friends are sent right from heaven above. . .
And thinking of you somehow makes me feel
That God is love and He's very real.

STRANGERS ARE FRIENDS
WE HAVEN'T MET

God knows no strangers, He loves us all,
The poor, the rich, the great, the small.
He is a friend who is always there
To share our troubles and lessen our care.
For no one is a stranger in God's sight,
For God is love, and in His light
May we, too, try in our small way
To make new friends from day to day.
So pass no stranger with an unseeing eye,
For God may be sending a new friend by.

GIVING IS THE
KEY TO LIVING

*E*very day is a reason for giving
And giving is the key to living. . .
So let us give ourselves away,
Not just today but every day,
And remember, a kind and thoughtful deed
Or a hand outstretched in a time of need
Is the rarest of gifts, for it is a part
Not of the purse but a loving heart. . .
And he who gives of himself will find
True joy of heart and peace of mind.

COUNTING
BLESSINGS

THANK YOU, GOD, FOR EVERYTHING

Thank You, God, for everything—
the big things and the small—
For every good gift comes from God,
the Giver of them all,
And all too often we accept
without any thanks or praise
The gifts God sends as blessings
each day in many ways.
And so at this time we offer up a prayer
To thank You, God, for giving us
a lot more than our share.
First, thank You for the little things
that often come our way—
The things we take for granted
and don't mention when we pray—
Oh make us more aware, dear God,
of little daily graces
That come to us with sweet surprise
from never-dreamed-of places.
And help us to remember
that the key to life and living
Is to make each prayer a prayer of thanks
and each day a day of thanksgiving.

THERE ARE BLESSINGS IN EVERYTHING

Blessings come in many guises
That God alone in love devises.
And sickness, which we dread so much,
Can bring a very healing touch,
For often on the wings of pain
The peace we sought before in vain
Will come to us with sweet surprise,
For God is merciful and wise. . .
And through long hours of tribulation
God gives us time for meditation,
And no sickness can be counted loss
That teaches us to bear our cross.

ADVERSITY CAN DISTRESS US OR BLESS US

*E*verything God sends to us,
no matter in what form,
Is sent with plan and purpose,
for by the fierceness of a storm
The atmosphere is changed and cleared
and the earth is washed and clean,
And the high winds of adversity
can make restless souls serene.
And while it's very difficult
for mankind to understand
God's intentions and His purpose
and the workings of His hand,
If we observe the miracles
that happen every day,
We cannot help but be convinced
that in His wondrous way
God makes what seemed unbearable
and painful and distressing
Easily acceptable when
we view it as a blessing.

THE FIRST THING EVERY MORNING, AND THE LAST THING EVERY NIGHT

Were you too busy this morning
to quietly stop and pray?
Did you hurry and drink your coffee
then frantically rush away,
Consoling yourself by saying,
God will always be there
Waiting to hear my petitions,
ready to answer each prayer?
It's true that the great, generous Savior
forgives our transgressions each day
And patiently waits for lost sheep
who constantly seem to stray,
But moments of prayer once omitted
in the busy rush of the day
Can never again be recaptured,
for they silently slip away.
For only through prayer that's unhurried
can the needs of the day be met,
And only through prayers said at evening
can we sleep without fears or regret.
So seek the Lord in the morning
and never forget Him at night,
For prayer is an unfailing blessing
that makes every burden seem light.

A Thankful Heart

Take nothing for granted, for whenever you do,
The joy of enjoying is lessened for you.
For we rob our own lives much more than we know
When we fail to respond or in any way show
Our thanks for the blessings that daily are ours—
The warmth of the sun, the fragrance of flowers,
The beauty of twilight, the freshness of dawn,
The coolness of dew on a green velvet lawn,
The kind little deeds so thoughtfully done,
The favors of friends and the love that someone
Unselfishly gives us in a myriad of ways,
Expecting no payment and no words of praise.
For the joy of enjoying and the fullness of living
Are found in the heart
that is filled with thanksgiving.

Not by Chance or Happenstance

Into our lives come many things
to break the dull routine—
The things we had not planned on
that happen unforeseen,
The unexpected little joys that
are scattered on our way,
Success we did not count on
or a rare, fulfilling day. . .
Now some folks call it fickle fate,
and some folks call it chance,
While others just accept it
as a pleasant happenstance.
But no matter what you call it,
it didn't come without design,
For all our lives are fashioned
by the hand that is divine,
And every lucky happening
and every lucky break
Are little gifts from God above
that are ours to freely take.

BLESSINGS DEVISED
BY GOD

*G*od speaks to us in many ways,
Altering our lives, our plans, and our days,
And His blessings come in many guises
That He alone in love devises,
And sorrow, which we dread so much,
Can bring a very healing touch. . .
For when we fail to heed His voice,
We leave the Lord no other choice
Except to use a firm, stern hand
To make us know He's in command. . .
For on the wings of loss and pain,
The peace we often sought in vain
Will come to us with sweet surprise,
For God is merciful and wise. . .
And through dark hours of tribulation
God gives us time for meditation,
And nothing can be counted loss
Which teaches us to bear our cross.

BEYOND OUR ASKING

*M*ore than hearts can imagine
or minds comprehend,
God's bountiful gifts are ours without end.
We ask for a cupful when the vast sea is ours;
We pick a small rosebud from a garden of flowers.
Whatever we ask for falls short of God's giving,
For His greatness exceeds every facet of living,
And always God's ready and eager and willing
To pour out His mercy, completely fulfilling
All of man's needs for peace, joy, and rest,
For God gives His children whatever is best.
Pleasures that never grow worn out and faded
And leave us depleted, disillusioned, and jaded—
For God has a storehouse just filled to the brim
With all that man needs, if we'll only ask Him.

THINGS TO BE
THANKFUL FOR

The good, green earth beneath our feet,
The air we breathe, the food we eat,
Some work to do, a goal to win,
A hidden longing deep within
That spurs us on to bigger things
And helps us meet what each day brings—
All these things and many more
Are things we should be thankful for. . .
And most of all, our thankful prayers
Should rise to God because He cares.

BLESSINGS COME
IN MANY GUISES

When troubles come and things go wrong
And days are cheerless and nights are long,
We find it so easy to give in to despair
By magnifying the burdens we bear.
We add to our worries by refusing to try
To look for the rainbow in an overcast sky,
And the blessings God sent in a darkened disguise
Our troubled hearts fail to recognize,
Not knowing God sent it not to distress us
But to strengthen our faith
and redeem us and bless us.

EXPECTATION! ANTICIPATION! REALIZATION!

God gives us a power we so seldom employ,
For we're so unaware it is filled with such joy.
The gift that God gives us is anticipation,
Which we can fulfill with sincere expectation,
For there's power in belief when we think we will find
Joy for the heart and peace for the mind,
And believing the day will bring a surprise
Is not only pleasant but surprisingly wise. . .
For we open the door to let joy walk through
When we learn to expect the best and the most, too,
And believing we'll find a happy surprise
Makes reality out of a fancied surmise.

FOREVER THANKS

*G*ive thanks for the blessings
that daily are ours—
The warmth of the sun,
the fragrance of flowers.
With thanks for all the thoughtful,
caring things you always do
And a loving wish for happiness
today and all year through!

Showers of Blessings

Each day there are showers of blessings
sent from the Father above,
For God is a great, lavish giver,
and there is no end to His love. . .
And His grace is more than sufficient;
His mercy is boundless and deep,
And His infinite blessings are countless,
and all this we're given to keep
If we but seek God and find Him
and ask for a bounteous measure
Of this wholly immeasurable offering
from God's inexhaustible treasure. . .
For no matter how big man's dreams are,
God's blessings are infinitely more,
For always God's giving is greater
than what man is asking for.

It's a
Wonderful
World

IT'S A WONDERFUL WORLD

*I*n spite of the fact we complain and lament
And view this old world with much discontent,
Deploring conditions and grumbling because
There's so much injustice and so many flaws,
It's a wonderful world, and it's people like you
Who make it that way by the things that they do.
For a warm, ready smile or a kind, thoughtful deed
Or a hand outstretched in an hour of need
Can change our whole outlook
and make the world bright,
Where a minute before just nothing seemed right.
It's a wonderful world and it always will be
If we keep our eyes open and focused to see
The wonderful things we are capable of
When we open our hearts to God and His love.

AFTER EACH STORM OF LIFE, THERE'S THE RAINBOW OF HOPE

*Th*e rainbow is God's promise
of hope for you and me,
And though the clouds hang heavy
and the sun we cannot see,
We know above the dark clouds
that fill the stormy sky
Hope's rainbow will come shining through
when the clouds have drifted by.

THE MYSTERY AND MIRACLE
OF HIS CREATIVE HAND

In the beauty of a snowflake
falling softly on the land
Is the mystery and the miracle
of God's great, creative hand.
What better answers are there
to prove His holy being
Than the wonders all around us
that are ours just for the seeing?

IN GOD'S TOMORROW THERE IS ETERNAL SPRING

All nature heeds the call of spring
as God awakens everything,
And all that seemed so dead and still
experiences a sudden thrill.
Oh, the joy in standing by
to watch a sapphire springtime sky
Or see a fragile flower break through
what just a day ago or two
Seemed barren ground still hard with frost,
for in God's world, no life is lost.
And flowers sleep beneath the ground,
but when they hear spring's waking sound,
They push themselves through layers of clay
to reach the sunlight of God's day.
And man and woman, like flowers, too,
must sleep until called from the darkened deep
To live in that place where angels sing
and where there is eternal spring.

My Garden of Prayer

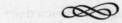

My garden beautifies my yard
and adds fragrance to the air,
But it is also my cathedral
and my quiet place of prayer.
So little do we realize
that the glory and the power
Of Him who made the universe
lies hidden in a flower!

THERE IS NO DEATH

There is no night without a dawning,
no winter without a spring,
And beyond death's dark horizon,
our hearts once more will sing.
For those who leave us for a while
have only gone away
Out of a restless, careworn world
into a brighter day,
Where there will be no partings
and time is not counted by years,
Where there are no trials or troubles,
no worries, no cares, and no tears.

THE SOUL, LIKE NATURE,
HAS SEASONS, TOO

When you feel cast down and despondently sad
And you long to be happy and carefree and glad,
Do you ask yourself, as I so often do,
Why must there be days that are cheerless and blue?
Why is the song silenced in the heart that was gay?
And then I ask God what makes life this way,
And His explanation makes everything clear—
The soul has its seasons the same as the year.
And oh, what a comfort to know there are reasons
That souls, like nature, must too have their seasons—
Bounteous seasons and barren ones, too,
Times for rejoicing and times to be blue. . .
And it takes a mixture of both bitter and sweet
To season our lives and make them complete.

AFTER THE WINTER GOD
SENDS THE SPRING

Springtime is a season
of hope and joy and cheer—
There's beauty all around us
to see and touch and hear. . .
So no matter how downhearted
and discouraged we may be,
New hope is born when we behold
leaves budding on a tree
Or when we see a timid flower
push through the frozen sod
And open wide in glad surprise
its petaled eyes to God. . .
For this is just God saying,
"Lift up your eyes to Me,
And the bleakness of your spirit,
like the budding springtime tree,
Will lose its wintry darkness
and your heavy heart will sing."
For God never sends the winter
without the joy of spring.

SPRING AWAKENS WHAT AUTUMN PUTS TO SLEEP

A garden of asters in varying hues,
Crimson pinks and violet blues,
Blossoming in the hazy fall,
Wrapped in autumn's lazy pall. . .
But early frost stole in one night,
And like a chilling, killing blight,
It touched each pretty aster's head,
And now the garden's still and dead,
And all the lovely flowers that bloomed
Will soon be buried and entombed
In winter's icy shroud of snow. . .
But oh, how wonderful to know
That after winter comes the spring
To breathe new life in everything,
For in God's plan both men and flowers
Can only reach bright, shining hours
By dying first to rise in glory
And prove again the Easter story.

EACH SPRING GOD RENEWS HIS PROMISE

Long, long ago in a land far away,
There came the dawn of the first Easter day,
And each year we see the promise reborn
That God gave the world on that first Easter morn.
For in each waking flower and each singing bird,
The promise of Easter is witnessed and heard,
And spring is God's way of speaking to men
And renewing the promise of Easter again. . .
So why should we grieve when our loved ones die,
For we'll meet them again in a cloudless sky.
For Easter is more than a beautiful story—
It's the promise of life and eternal glory.

ALL NATURE PROCLAIMS
ETERNAL LIFE

Flowers sleeping 'neath the snow,
Awakening when the spring winds blow,
Leafless trees so bare before
Gowned in lacy green once more,
Hard, unyielding, frozen sod
Now softly carpeted by God,
Still streams melting in the spring
Rippling over rocks that sing,
Barren, windswept, lonely hills
Turning gold with daffodils—
These miracles are all around
Within our sight and touch and sound,
As true and wonderful today
As when the stone was rolled away,
Proclaiming to all doubting men
That in God all things live again.

APRIL

April comes with cheeks a-glowing;
Silver streams are all a-flowing;
Flowers open wide their eyes
In lovely rapturous surprise.
Lilies dream beside the brooks,
Violets in meadow nooks,
And the birds gone wild with glee
Fill the woods with melody.

LIFE'S GOLDEN AUTUMN

*M*emory opens wide the door
on a happy day like this,
And with a sweet nostalgia
we longingly recall,
The happy days of long ago
that seem the best of all. . .
But time cannot be halted
in its swift and endless flight,
And age is sure to follow youth
as day comes after night,
And once again it's proven
that the restless brain of man
Is powerless to alter
God's great, unchanging plan. . .
But while our steps grow slower
and we grow more tired, too,
The soul goes roaring upward
to realms untouched and new,
Where God's children live forever
in the beauty of His love.

FAITH AND HOPE

WITH GOD ALL
THINGS ARE POSSIBLE

*N*othing is ever too hard to do
If your faith is strong and your purpose is true. . .
So never give up, and never stop—
Just journey on to the mountaintop!

We Can't, but God Can

Why things happen as they do
we do not always know,
And we cannot always fathom why
our spirits sink so low.
We flounder in our dark distress;
we are wavering and unstable,
But when we're most inadequate,
the Lord God's always able—
For though we are incapable,
God's powerful and great,
And there's no darkness of the mind
God cannot penetrate. . .
And while He may not instantly
unravel all the strands
Of the tangled thoughts that trouble us,
He completely understands—
And in His time, if we have faith,
He will gradually restore
The brightness to our spirits
that we've been longing for. . .
So remember there's no cloud too dark
for God's light to penetrate
If we keep on believing
and have faith enough to wait.

Do You Believe?

When the way seems long and the day is dark
And we can't hear the sound of the thrush or the lark
And our hearts are heavy with worry and care
And we are lost in the depths of despair,
That is the time when faith alone
Can lead us out of the dark unknown. . .
For faith to believe when the way is rough
And faith to hang on when the going is tough
Will never fail to pull us through
And bring us strength and comfort, too. . .
For all we really ever need
Is faith as a grain of mustard seed,
For all God asks is Do you believe?
For if you do ye shall receive.

TRUST GOD

Take heart and meet each minute
with faith in God's great love,
Aware that every day of life
is controlled by God above. . .
And never dread tomorrow
or what the future brings—
Just pray for strength and courage
and trust God in all things.

FINDING FAITH
IN A FLOWER

*S*ometimes when faith is running low
And I cannot fathom why things are so,
I walk among the flowers that grow
And learn the answers to all I would know...
For among my flowers I have come to see
Life's miracle and its mystery,
And standing in silence and reverie,
My faith comes flooding back to me.

A Child's Faith

*J*esus loves me, this I know,
For the Bible tells me so. . ."
Little children ask no more,
For love is all they're looking for,
And in a small child's shining eyes
The faith of all the ages lies. . .
For faith in things we cannot see
Requires a child's simplicity. . .
For lost in life's complexities,
We drift upon uncharted seas,
And slowly faith disintegrates
While wealth and power accumulate. . .
And in his arrogance and pride,
No longer is man satisfied
To place his confidence and love
With childlike faith in God above. . .
Oh, heavenly Father, grant again
A simple, childlike faith to men,
And with a small child's trusting eyes,
May all men come to realize
That faith alone can save man's soul
And lead him to a higher goal.

FAITH AND TRUST

Sometimes when a light
Goes out of our lives
And we are left in darkness
And we do not know which way to go,
We must put our hand
Into the hand of God
And ask Him to lead us.
And if we let our lives become a prayer
Until we are strong enough
To stand under the weight
Of our own thoughts again,
Somehow, even the most difficult
Hours are bearable.

GOD IS THE ANSWER

We read the headlines daily,
and we listen to the news;
We are anxious and bewildered
with the world's conflicting views. . .
So instead of reading headlines
that disturb the heart and mind,
Let us open up the Bible,
for in doing so we'll find
That this age is no different
from the millions gone before,
And in every hour of crisis
God has opened up a door.
And though there's hate and violence
and dissension all around,
We can always find a refuge
that is built on solid ground.
So as we pray for guidance,
may a troubled world revive
Faith in God and confidence
so our nation may survive
And draw us ever closer
to God and to each other
Until every stranger is a friend
and every man a brother.

HELP US TO SEE
AND UNDERSTAND

God, give us wider vision to see and understand
That both the sunshine and the showers
are gifts from Thy great hand.
And teach us that it takes the showers
to make the flowers grow,
And only in the storms of life
when the winds of trouble blow
Can man, too, reach maturity
and grow in faith and grace
And gain the strength and courage
to enable him to face
Sunny days as well as rain,
high peaks as well as low,
Knowing that the April showers
will make May flowers grow. . .
And then at last may we accept
the sunshine and the showers,
Confident it takes them both
to make salvation ours.

THIS, TOO, WILL
PASS AWAY

If I can endure for this minute
whatever is happening to me
No matter how heavy my heart is
or how dark the moment might be—
If I can remain calm and quiet
with all my world crashing about me,
Secure in the knowledge God loves me
when everyone else seems to doubt me—
If I can but keep on believing
what I know in my heart to be true,
That darkness will fade with the morning
and that this will pass away, too—
Then nothing in life can defeat me,
for as long as this knowledge remains,
I can suffer whatever is happening,
for I know God will break all the chains
That are binding me tight in the darkness
and trying to fill me with fear. . .
For there is no night without dawning,
and I know that my morning is near.

FAITH IS A MOVER OF MOUNTAINS

Faith is a force that is greater
than knowledge or power or skill,
And the darkest defeat turns to triumph
if you trust in God's wisdom and will,
For faith is a mover of mountains—
there's nothing man cannot achieve
If he has the courage to try it
and then has the faith to believe.

FAITH IS A MIGHTY FORTRESS

*W*e look ahead through each changing year
With mixed emotions of hope and fear—
Unwilling to trust in the Father's will,
We count on our logic and shadow skill,
And in our arrogance and pride,
We are no longer satisfied.
Oh, heavenly Father, grant again
A simple, childlike faith to men,
Forgetting color, race, and creed
And seeing only the heart's deep need.
For faith alone can save man's soul
And lead him to a higher goal,
For there's but one unfailing course—
We win by faith and not by force.

WHAT MORE
CAN YOU ASK?

God's love endures forever—
what a wonderful thing to know
When the tides of life run against you
and your spirit is downcast and low.
God's kindness is ever around you
always ready to freely impart
Strength to your faltering spirit,
cheer to your lonely heart.
God's presence is ever beside you,
as near as the reach of your hand.
You have but to tell Him your troubles—
there is nothing He won't understand. . .
And knowing God's love is unfailing,
and His mercy unending and great,
You have but to trust in His promise,
"God comes not too soon or too late". . .
So wait with a heart that is patient
for the goodness of God to prevail,
For never do prayers go unanswered,
and His mercy and love never fail.

THE GREAT TOMORROW

*T*here is always a tomorrow.
Tomorrow belongs as much to you as it does to me.
The dawn of a new day means the dawn of a new life.
We cannot peer into its storehouse, but the
very impenetrable mystery which enwraps the
ever-approaching tomorrow is the one thing that
keeps the fires of hope constantly burning.
Even if our today is filled with sadness and defeat,
who can foretell what the next day will bring to us?
Let us all eagerly await what destiny will deal us.
We speak of man meeting his fate, and we speak
truthfully, for every day we see life converged to life.
Tomorrow may hold your fate; tomorrow may
mean your victory. The great joy of expectation, the
wonderment of an unknown realm, the splendor
of the vast, unlimitable future all lie in the eternal
tomorrow, the day which makes life worth living.

COMFORT IN THE
FACE OF LOSS

ONLY GOD

At times like these
Man is helpless. . .
It is only God
Who can speak the words
That calm the sea,
Still the wind,
And ease the pain. . .
So lean on Him
And you will never walk alone.

THY WILL BE DONE

God did not promise sun without rain,
Light without darkness, or joy without pain.
He only promised strength for the day
When the darkness comes and we lose our way. . .
For only through sorrow do we grow more aware
That God is our refuge in times of despair.
But God seems much closer and needed much more
When trouble and sorrow stand outside our door,
For then we seek shelter in His wondrous love,
And we ask him to send us help from above. . .
And that is the reason we know it is true
That bright, shining hours and dark, sad ones, too,
Are part of the plan God made for each one,
And all we can pray is "Thy will be done."
And know that you are never alone,
For God is your Father, and you're one of His own.

DEEP IN MY HEART

*H*appy little memories
go flitting through my mind,
And in all my thoughts and memories
I always seem to find
The picture of your face, dear,
the memory of your touch,
And all the other little things
I've come to love so much.
You cannot go beyond my thoughts
or leave my love behind,
Because I keep you in my heart
and forever on my mind. . .
And though I may not tell you,
I think you know it's true
That I find daily happiness
in the very thought of you.

ON THE OTHER
SIDE OF DEATH

Death is a gateway we all must pass through
To reach that fair land where the soul's born anew,
For man's born to die, and his sojourn on earth
Is a short span of years beginning with birth.
And like pilgrims we wander until Death takes our hand
And we start on the journey to God's Promised Land,
A place where we'll find no suffering or tears,
Where time is not counted in days, months, or years.
And in that fair city that God has prepared
Are unending joys to be happily shared
With all of our loved ones who patiently wait
On death's other side to open the gate.

MY BIRTHDAY IN BETHESDA

How little we know what God has in store
As daily He blesses our lives more and more.
I've lived many years, and I've learned many things,
But today I have grown new spiritual wings. . .
For pain has a way of broadening our view
And bringing us closer in sympathy, too,
To those who are living in constant pain
And trying somehow to bravely sustain
The faith and endurance to keep on trying
When they almost welcome the peace of dying. . .
Without this experience I would have lived and died
Without fathoming the pain of Christ crucified,
For none of us knows what pain is all about
Until our spiritual wings start to sprout.
So thank You, God, for the gift You sent
To teach me that pain's heaven-sent.

NOTHING IS LOST FOREVER

*T*he waking earth in springtime
Reminds us it is true
That nothing ever really dies
That is not born anew. . .
So trust God's all-wise wisdom
And doubt the Father never,
For in His heavenly kingdom
There is nothing lost forever.

A MESSAGE OF CONSOLATION

On the wings of death and sorrow
God sends us new hope for tomorrow,
And in His mercy and His grace
He gives us strength to bravely face
The lonely days that stretch ahead
And to know our loved one is not dead
But only sleeping out of our sight,
And we'll meet in that land where there is no night.

THIS IS JUST
A RESTING PLACE

*S*ometimes the road of life seems long
as we travel through the years,
And with a heart that's broken
and eyes brimful of tears,
We falter in our weariness
and sink beside the way,
But God leans down and whispers,
"Child, there'll be another day."
And the road will grow much smoother
and much easier to face,
So do not be disheartened;
this is just a resting place.

The Home Beyond

We feel so sad when those we love
Are called to live in the home above,
But why should we grieve when they say good-bye
And go to dwell in a cloudless sky?
For they have but gone to prepare the way,
And we'll meet them again some happy day,
For God has told us that nothing can sever
A life He created to live forever.
So let God's promise soften our sorrow
And give us new strength for a brighter tomorrow.

Uplifting Optimism

BE OF GOOD CHEER,
THERE'S NOTHING TO FEAR

Cheerful thoughts, like sunbeams,
lighten up the darkest fears,
For when the heart is happy
there's just no time for tears,
And when the face is smiling,
it's impossible to frown,
And when you are high-spirited,
you cannot feel low-down. . .
For when the heart is cheerful,
it cannot be filled with fear,
And without fear, the way ahead
seems more distinct and clear,
And we realize there's nothing
that we must face alone,
For our heavenly Father loves us,
and our problems are His own.

MEET LIFE'S TRIALS WITH SMILES

There are times when life overwhelms us
and our trials seem too many to bear;
It is then we should stop to remember
God is standing by ready to share
The uncertain hours that confront us
and fill us with fear and despair,
For God in His goodness has promised
that the cross that He gives us to wear
Will never exceed our endurance
or be more than our strength can bear. . .
And secure in that blessed assurance,
we can smile as we face tomorrow,
For God holds the key to the future,
and no sorrow or care we need borrow.

MAKE YOUR DAY BRIGHT
BY THINKING RIGHT

Don't start your day by supposin'
that trouble is just ahead;
It's better to stop supposin'
and start with a prayer instead. . .
For what is the use of supposin'
that dire things could happen to you,
Worrying about some misfortune
that seldom if ever comes true. . .
But instead of just idle supposin',
step forward to meet each new day
Secure in the knowledge God's near you
to lead you each step of the way. . .
For supposin' the worst things will happen
only helps to make them come true,
And you darken the bright, happy moments
that the dear Lord has given to you. . .
So if you desire to be happy
and get rid of the misery of dread,
Just give up supposin' the worst things
and look for the best things instead.

Yesterday, Today, and Tomorrow

Yesterday's dead, tomorrow's unborn,
So there's nothing to fear and nothing to mourn,
For all that is past and all that has been
Can never return to be lived once again. . .
And what lies ahead or the things that will be
Are still in God's hands, so it is not up to me
To live in the future that is God's great unknown,
For the past and the present God claims for His own. . .
So all I need do is to live for today
And trust God to show me the truth and the way.
For it's only the memory of things that have been
And expecting tomorrow to bring trouble again
That fills my today, which God wants to bless,
With uncertain fears and borrowed distress. . .
For all I need live for is this one little minute,
For life's here and now and eternity's in it.

COUNT YOUR GAINS, NOT LOSSES

As we travel down life's busy road
Complaining of our heavy load,
We often think God's been unfair
And given us much more than our share
Of daily, little irritations
And disappointing tribulations.
We count our losses, not our gain,
And remember only tears and pain.
The good things we forget completely,
When God looked down and blessed us sweetly.
Our troubles fill our every thought;
We dwell upon the goals we sought,
And so we walk with heads held low,
And little do we guess or know
That someone near us on life's street
Is burdened deeply with defeat,
And if we'd but forget our care
And stop in sympathy to share
The burden that our brother carried,
Our minds and hearts would be less harried
And we would feel our load was small—
In fact, we carried no load at all.

LOOK ON THE SUNNY SIDE

There are always two sides—
the good and the bad,
The dark and the light,
the sad and the glad. . .
But in looking back over
the good and the bad,
We're aware of the number
of good things we've had.
So thank God for the good things
He has already done,
And be grateful to Him
for the battles you've won,
And know that the same God
who helped you before
Is ready and willing
to help you once more.
For our Father in heaven
always knows what is best,
And if you trust His wisdom,
your life will be blessed. . .
For always remember
that whatever betide you,
You are never alone,
for God is beside you.

BURDENS CAN
BE BLESSINGS

Our Father knows what's best for us,
So why should we complain—
We always want the sunshine,
But He knows there must be rain.
We love the sound of laughter
And the merriment of cheer,
But our hearts would lose their tenderness
If we never shed a tear. . .
So whenever we are troubled
And life has lost its song,
It's God testing us with burdens
Just to make our spirit strong!

GLORY TO GOD
IN THE HIGHEST

Glory to God in the highest, and on
earth peace, goodwill toward men."
May the angels' song of long ago
ring in our hearts again
And bring a new awareness
that the fate of every nation
Is sealed securely in the hand
of the Maker of creation. . .
For man, with all his knowledge,
his wisdom, and his skill,
Is powerless to go beyond
the holy Fathers' will. . .
And when we fully recognize
the helplessness of man
And seek our Father's guidance
in our every thought and plan,
Then only can we build a world
of faith and hope and love,
And only then can man achieve
the life he's dreaming of.

THE FRAGRANCE REMAINS

There's an old Chinese proverb
that if practiced each day
Would change the whole world in a wonderful way.
Its truth is so simple, it's easy to do,
And it works every time and successfully, too.
For you can't do a kindness without a reward
Not in silver nor gold but in joy from the Lord.
You can't light a candle to show others the way
Without feeling the warmth of that bright little ray,
And you can't pluck a rose all fragrant with dew
Without part of its fragrance remaining with you.

Wish Not for Ease or to Do as You Please

If wishes worked like magic
and plans worked that way, too,
And if everything you wished for,
whether good or bad for you,
Immediately were granted
with no effort on your part,
You'd experience no fulfillment
of your spirit or your heart. . .
For things achieved too easily
lose their charm and meaning, too,
For it is life's difficulties
and the trial times we go through
That make us strong in spirit
and endow us with the will
To surmount the insurmountable
and to climb the highest hill. . .
For to triumph over trouble
and grow stronger with defeat
Is to win the kind of victory
that will make your life complete.

Lives Distressed
Cannot Be Blessed

Refuse to be discouraged,
refuse to be distressed,
For when we are despondent,
our lives cannot be blessed.
For doubt and fear and worry
close the door to faith and prayer,
And there's no room for blessings
when we're lost in deep despair.
So remember when you're troubled
with uncertainty and doubt,
It is best to tell our Father
what our fear is all about,
For unless we seek His guidance
when troubled times arise,
We are bound to make decisions
that are twisted and unwise.
But when we view our problems
through the eyes of God above,
Misfortunes turn to blessings
and hatred turns to love.

CONCLUSION

And now that you've come to the end of this book,
Pause and reflect and take a swift backward look
And you'll find that to follow
God's commandment each day
Is not only the righteous and straight, narrow way
But a joyous experience, for there's many a thrill
In going God's way and in doing His will. . .
For in traveling God's way you are never alone,
For all of your problems God takes as His own,
And always He's ready to counsel and guide you,
And in sadness or gladness
He's always beside you. . .
And to live for God's glory and to walk in His truth
Brings peace to the angel and joy to the youth,
And at the end of life's journey,
there's His promised reward
Of life everlasting in the house of the Lord.

INDEX